The 7 Laws of Communication

The Secrets of Being Comfortable, Confident, And Unforgettable with Anyone!

FREE BONUS E-BOOK!

Body Language Mastery

How would you like to control your actions to the point where you are exuding confidence and belief in yourself? What about being able to help someone open up to you on an interview or a first date? Do you want to be able to create any type of positive reaction, without saying a word? Master human psychology by reading the way people behave with their bodies...

Briancagneey.com/BodyLanguageMasteryBook

© **Copyright 2016 by Brian Cagneey - All rights reserved.**

This document is geared towards providing exact and reliable information in regards to the topic and issue covered. The publication is sold with the idea that the publisher is not required to render accounting, officially permitted, or otherwise, qualified services. If advice is necessary, legal or professional, a practiced individual in the profession should be ordered.

- From a Declaration of Principles which was accepted and approved equally by a Committee of the American Bar Association and a Committee of Publishers and Associations.

In no way is it legal to reproduce, duplicate, or transmit any part of this document in either electronic means or in printed format. Recording of this publication is strictly prohibited and any storage of this document is not allowed unless with written permission from the publisher. All rights reserved.

The information provided herein is stated to be truthful and consistent, in that any liability, in terms of inattention or otherwise, by any usage or abuse of any policies, processes, or directions contained within is the solitary and utter responsibility of the recipient reader. Under no circumstances will any legal responsibility or blame be held against the publisher for any reparation, damages, or monetary loss due to the information herein, either directly or indirectly.

Respective authors own all copyrights not held by the publisher.

The information herein is offered for informational purposes solely, and is universal as so. The presentation of the information is without contract or any type of guarantee assurance.

The trademarks that are used are without any consent, and the publication of the trademark is without permission or backing by the trademark owner. All trademarks and brands within this book are for clarifying purposes only and are the owned by the owners themselves, not affiliated with this document.

Table Of Contents

FREE BONUS E-BOOK! 1

INTRODUCTION 4

1ST LAW OF COMMUNICATION: THE ONLY TIME YOU SHOULD THINK ABOUT YOURSELF IS WITH THIS ONE IDEA 5

2ND LAW OF COMMUNICATION: YOU HAVE ALREADY LOST IF YOU DO THIS, THIS, AND THAT... 8

3RD LAW OF COMMUNICATION: A CRAZY SIMPLE ACTION THAT MAKES YOU AND EVERYONE FEEL A LOT BETTER 11

4TH LAW OF COMMUNICATION: HOW TO TAP INTO SOMEONE'S STRONGEST DESIRE WITHOUT MANIPULATING ANYONE 14

5TH LAW OF COMMUNICATION: IF YOU DO THIS ONE THING, PEOPLE WILL NATURALLY THINK YOU ARE GREAT 16

6TH LAW OF COMMUNICATION: HOW TO SEEM CLEVER WITHOUT SAYING A SINGLE WORD 19

7TH LAW OF COMMUNICATION: FOLLOW THIS IF YOU WANT TO RESOLVE ANY CONFLICT 22

CONCLUSION 26

FREE BONUS E-BOOK! 27

OTHER BOOKS IN THE "7 LAWS" SERIES 28

Introduction

I want to thank and congratulate you for purchasing the book *The 7 Laws of Communication: The Secrets of Being Comfortable, Confident And Unforgettable with Anyone!*

This book contains detailed steps in how to assert yourself in social communication. Whether you're with friends or strangers, new or familiar, you can read this book in confidence knowing you'll learn how to present yourself better verbally.

Here's an inescapable fact: communication is all about social interaction. It's alright to be shy around others, but this book is meant to help build self-confidence and engagement with anyone you meet. You'll need it when building intimate relationships with friends, family or significant others. You'll need it for jobs as well, whether it's fast-food, retail or a big corporate business.

It's time to learn the seven laws of communication, starting now!

1st Law of Communication: The Only Time You Should Think About Yourself Is with This One Idea

As a general rule in communication, you should always try to maintain your focus on the other person. This one principle can help you look and feel more confident. There is one exception to this rule. The only time you should think about yourself during any communication with others is regarding your attitude and your actions. Both your internal attitudes and the small external actions you do, display your overall feeling about yourself and the other person.

Attitude

Others usually accept you based on your own evaluation of yourself. Many times, how others treat you is reflected in the attitude you have towards yourself. If you think you are a nobody, people will probably treat you as such. If you are confident, your communication is bound to come out that way. It is one of the more difficult tasks to be able to change your attitude about yourself and your expectations about your interactions with others. Rest assured, your attitude about your ability to communicate and how you feel about yourself is far more important than most people realize. If you can begin to change your attitude about yourself, you will naturally start to communicate better with others as your confidence grows.

Here are just a few ways you can start to develop a better attitude about yourself:

1. Affirmations – Affirmation phrases you tell yourself as a form of self coaching are meant to charge you up and boost your conviction to follow through in your actions. When repeated several times each day, affirmations can reprogram your subconscious with positive thinking. If done properly, this triggers positive feelings that drive you to do better.

2. Visualization – Studies of psychology indicate that great athletes, surgeons, engineers and artists use affirmations and visualizations to bolster their skill sets. For example, Nelson Mandela admitted how visualization helped him stay positive while imprisoned for 27 years. He thought continually of the day he could walk free and fantasized of what he would like to do when that day came. You can do the same. Visualize yourself being confident in your interactions with others. See yourself

smiling and enjoying each conversation. Do your best to actually imagine the feeling of being confident and feeling good about yourself. This will help you to grow your confidence.

3. Positive Self Talk – Self talk is a way to override past negative thoughts and replace or erase them with conscious, positive ones. Those new conscious thoughts act like a seed to reprogram your brain and behavior to match the positive attitude. Positive self-talk takes time, because you have to train yourself to notice what you are actually saying to yourself in your inner monologue. Self-talk is a discipline and unlike intentional reading affirmations, self-talk requires more of an ongoing observation and practice at any moment.

4. Watch Your Words – Remember when your parents warned you to be careful of what you put on the internet? Your spoken words are the same thing; once you say it out to the world, everyone knows and you can't take it back. What you say aloud reflects what you believe in your heart, based on all the things you have come to believe about yourself. Like self-talk, always be mindful of the words you say when talking to others.

Actions

Although "actions speak louder than words," is usually the case, when it comes to communication, both actions and words are on the same level. Your actions in any interaction will always be determined by the attitude you have towards it. So, first and foremost, assume you will have a friendly reaction! Assume the other person will like you and your interaction can be a lot less awkward. There certainly isn't a 100% guarantee that the other person will be friendly, but your attitude can make a huge difference in putting you at ease, which in turn can make the other person feel comfortable. Remember, your expectations in any communication go a long way in predicting the outcome; so keep your expectations positive.

In addition to having a positive attitude and expectation towards the other person, there are several actions you can take to make sure you feel comfortable, the other person feels comfortable and you leave a conversation feeling confident:

1. You Have to Start Somewhere – You have to engage in small talk. Most people don't want to do that. Lots of people want to avoid feeling awkward and get to more meaningful conversation. You will never get

to that point if you don't first engage in small talk. Basic, surface level questions are what help people open up. It gets the ball rolling. From there, the conversation can build momentum. You can find connections, hear interesting stories and learn fun facts about the other person. People love to talk about themselves, so just push through the initial small talk and the conversation will soon be flowing naturally.

2. Act Confidently – This is directly related to your attitude. Even if you have to "fake it before you make it," you'll be surprised by how quickly your natural confidence can take over. Act as if the person you are about to talk with will enjoy your company and conversation. When you approach any conversation with confidence and combine that with basic small talk, it's amazing how you can feel after you leave the conversation. Just focus on acting confidently and your actions will soon follow. Faking it until you feel confident puts your mind on a positive outcome, rather than a fearful one. This alone can boost your confidence.

3. Positive Greeting – People tend to love working and living with others that enjoy life for what it is. People also appreciate others when they go out of their way to make them happy. It can be as simple as a positive greeting with a smile. This simple action can set the tone for the entire conversation. If you can act confidently and develop just enough courage to put a smile on your face and say hello, it can dramatically alter the start of your interactions. You're setting up the entire conversation to be a positive experience for you and the other person. This can trigger a ripple effect of positive actions towards others for the rest of the day and beyond.

4. Be Enthusiastic– Enthusiasm is to attitude what breathing is to life. When you are enthusiastic, you apply what you have more efficiently through commitment, determination and spirit. You put yourself in motion, have the spirit to go through with your actions and believe you are doing the right thing. To have enthusiasm is to have one of the most empowering character traits ever.

Actions and attitude make all the difference. If you can apply just this first law to all your communication with others, you are on your way to being more comfortable, confident and unforgettable with everyone you meet!

2nd Law of Communication: You Have Already Lost If You Do This, This, And That…

Learning to communicate in a way that makes you stand out is as much about what not to do, as it is what to do. In everyday conversations, whether with strangers or with friends, one of the most difficult things to do is to steer clear of those little habits that are so easy to fall into. Everyone has participated in these subtle, but often negative communication traits at some point in their life. Although it is incredibly easy to fall into these habits, it is vital that you learn to control these natural impulses to help you be more confident and likeable.

Don't Complain

Complaining is the easiest thing for you to do when you are in any conversation. It is much easier to focus on the negative than the positive. This urge needs to be fought.

Complaining is usually a negative opinion you have. Most people will judge you based on your opinions, which means if you have a lot of negative opinions to share, you'll most likely find yourself alone in a crowd. A giant list of negative opinions creates a giant negative atmosphere for anyone that comes in contact with you. Most people simply do not want to be around that, especially meeting a new acquaintance. Think about how you would react if the person you just met started listing all their complaints about people, places and other things in life? What are the chances they would be complaining about you to someone else down the road? Remember back in the last chapter when we talked about attitude; your attitude in general will go a long way in determining your interactions with new people and new friends. If you have a negative attitude because of all your complaints, people will pick up on that. Most people want to be happy, and unless they are miserable as well, they won't want to be a part of a lot of negative talk. You will be amazed at how much you can set yourself apart just by lessening the amount of complaining you do with others.

Don't Criticize or Condemn

An equally hard challenge is to avoid criticizing or condemning others. This is extremely difficult when it comes to differences in opinion. It is perfectly alright to have a different opinion than someone else, but, when your convictions boil over into criticism or condemnation, it can easily lead to a broken relationship.

Now, there is certainly a difference between criticism that is constructive and criticism that is destructive. Destructive criticism usually focuses on the person, rather than the action and how to work through any differences or miscommunication. A destructive critic is also wrapped in potentially negative emotions, such as anger or hatred. Constructive criticism is usually based on the idea of helping resolve a problem that needs to be fixed. It's focused more on the action, in a calm, non-threatening way. Everyone who has ever experienced any sort of feedback can certainly tell the difference between constructive and destructive criticism.

Condemnation is very similar to criticism, in that it also focuses on the person and the wrong that was committed. A big difference between the two is that condemnation usually drives home the blame and criticizes the person for something they know was their fault, but was simply a mistake. With criticism, there may be a mistake, and some potential ignorance or miscommunication on the other person's part. With condemnation, the person knows they made a mistake, but you make them feel even worse about it.

Avoid Arguing, Teasing and Sarcasm

It's important to limit and avoid arguing, teasing and sarcasm. Arguments will happen, as no one is perfect and people disagree, but it's necessary for you to not make arguing with others a second nature. There is a famous story about Benjamin Frankin, America's great inventor and diplomat who helped bring freedom to the United States. At a young age, it was said that he was so argumentative with everyone he met, that people would actually cross the road when they saw him approaching! Franklin was brilliant, but his wisdom and knowledge were used to fight everyone's opinion and no one liked him. We all know that Franklin changed his ways, but if that was his story, wouldn't you think you could also have the same story? Constantly arguing every little point someone brings up is a sure fire way to have people dislike you and a great way to spend a lot of your time alone. Debate and civil discussion certainly have their place, but have discernment to know the appropriate place and time.

Teasing is often done in good fun. Although it may seem harmless, constant teasing can have severe negative consequences. Very often, we don't know what's going on in someone's mind when they are being teased. They may look like they are okay with it, but many times they aren't. Continuous teasing can send very negative messages to the person being teased. Similar to how our own words can affect our attitude and well-being, the words we say to others can have a just as powerful, if not more of an affect. Hearing the same teasing over and over can lead that person to actually believe what you are saying is true. Imagine how destructive that could be to someone if they started to actually believe those things you teased them about. This could seriously damage a person long after the teasing has stopped.

Sarcasm should be handled exactly like teasing. Sarcastic comments are also said in fun, but like teasing, can have similar affects. Sarcasm is usually a defense mechanism to lessen the severity of an issue. A sarcastic comment may tell another person that you don't really care about what they are saying. It also can cause the other person to become defensive and on edge. Manyarguments have started over one simple, seemingly harmless, sarcastic comment. Be sure to monitor your words and be mindful to limit sarcasm. Most of the time it does more damage than intended.

At the end of the day, it goes back to our attitudes and our actions. We have to possess enough self-awareness to see how our words can affect not only ourselves, but the people around us as well. It's not an easy job to become more mindful of those bad communication habits that are so ingrained in us, but with time, patience and intentionality, the road to positive communication and confidence with others will become easier and easier.

3rd Law of Communication: A Crazy Simple Action That Makes You and Everyone Feel a Lot Better

This is the simplest thing you can do to boost your communication skills, and its shocking how many people don't do it! Kids and little children do this often, even some of your pets seem to be able to pull this off; but walk down the street and look at the majority of people; they'll have their eyes forward and faces straight. We're talking about the easy to do communication skill of smiling. Yes, smiling.

Smiling is a great way to leave a positive impression on others you communicate with. To smile is to be confident and this helps anyone you meet to automatically feel more comfortable. Smiling is a way to help put everyone around you at ease. It's even scientifically proven that smiling has a tremendous positive effect on you, as well as others around you.

The Science Behind Smiling

Smiling literally makes you happy. Researchers at the University of Munich used an MRI machine to measure the emotional processing receptors in the brain. They first measured people that smiled naturally. Then they took the second group, injected Botox into their cheeks to prevent them from smiling, and then again measure their brains. The scientists found that just the physical act of smiling actually activated the emotional happiness circuits in the brain!

Additional data showed that smiling was crucial in forming relationships. Individuals with brain lesions, physical malfunctions, physiological disorders and other similar conditions that led to the loss of facial control had more difficulty forming substantive relationships because they couldn't control the muscles to smile. Smiling is the first ingredient that brings two people together.

Having a smile on your face not only makes you happy, but also makes others happy as well. Researchers from Sweden exposed study participants to real and genuine smiles and measured their reactions. They found that genuine smiles received directly induced smiles from the participants. Smiling is contagious.

4th Law of Communication: How to Tap into Someone's Strongest Desire Without Manipulating Anyone

Many of these communication laws seemed to be common sense. How come more people don't actually use these laws to help them be more comfortable and confident with others? It's because even common sense principles need to be repeated over and over in order to sink in. This fourth law of communication is maybe the most important one to repeat if you want to succeed in communicating naturally and confidently.

Give Honest and Sincere Appreciation

Every single human being has a strong desire to feel approved and to feel important. It's one of the strongest desires of all humans: the need to feel special in some kind of way. When it comes to making people feel important and special, giving honest and sincere appreciation is the way to go.

When you're honest and sincere in showing appreciation for someone, you are speaking from your heart. It's natural and not forced. Everyone has a built in "sincerity meter" and they can tell when you are just trying to flatter them. This can be a turn off when communicating with someone. But, if the appreciation is sincere, it will do wonders in making them feel special and valued. This in turn will give them a great impression of you and can really help in developing the conversation or even developing the relationship. Sincere praise will energize anyone you speak with.

Be an Observer

The key to living out this law is becoming more observant of others and listening to them.

You will have to become a natural observer of people as they tell you their story. You have to be willing to listen to them. Everyone loves to talk about themselves and if you can pinpoint just one little thing you can praise them on, it will be amazing to see the results. Being observant and appreciating or praising them for something is one of the strongest ways to boost someone's confidence.

4th Law of Communication: How to Tap into Someone's Strongest Desire Without Manipulating Anyone

Many of these communication laws seemed to be common sense. How come more people don't actually use these laws to help them be more comfortable and confident with others? It's because even common sense principles need to be repeated over and over in order to sink in. This fourth law of communication is maybe the most important one to repeat if you want to succeed in communicating naturally and confidently.

Give Honest and Sincere Appreciation

Every single human being has a strong desire to feel approved and to feel important. It's one of the strongest desires of all humans: the need to feel special in some kind of way. When it comes to making people feel important and special, giving honest and sincere appreciation is the way to go.

When you're honest and sincere in showing appreciation for someone, you are speaking from your heart. It's natural and not forced. Everyone has a built in "sincerity meter" and they can tell when you are just trying to flatter them. This can be a turn off when communicating with someone. But, if the appreciation is sincere, it will do wonders in making them feel special and valued. This in turn will give them a great impression of you and can really help in developing the conversation or even developing the relationship. Sincere praise will energize anyone you speak with.

Be an Observer

The key to living out this law is becoming more observant of others and listening to them.

You will have to become a natural observer of people as they tell you their story. You have to be willing to listen to them. Everyone loves to talk about themselves and if you can pinpoint just one little thing you can praise them on, it will be amazing to see the results. Being observant and appreciating or praising them for something is one of the strongest ways to boost someone's confidence.

- Smiling is contagious and makes others happy

- You position yourself for more success in life and your long term relationships

- When you smile, you are that much more confident and approachable to others

An Experiment

Here's an experiment for you to try:

Go out for a walk, and whenever you see someone, greet them with a smile. Maybe wave, say "hello", shake their hand or offer to help them when they look like they're struggling with something heavy. As long as you greet them with a smile, it counts. Try to see how many people smile back, appreciating the gesture as you spread a little happiness.

In a 30-yearlong study, psychologist Dacher Keltner of the University of California-Berkeley examined the smiles of students in yearbooks and measured their success and well-being as time progressed. Keltner and his colleagues found that those that smiled more and scored well on happiness tests had long and fulfilling marriages. They were among the participants with wide, genuine smiles.

As you can see, the simple action of smiling can go a long way in helping you to be more confident and have more rewarding relationships. You have the opportunity to spread happiness and make others feel good with just a genuine smile.

As easy as putting a smile on your face is, why do so many people struggle to do it? We have all been walking down the street and seen the faces of people walking by us. Or maybe we have been in an elevator with someone and seen the stern look on their face. Why is that so prevalent in our culture?

Maybe it is because smiling requires a different mindset. You have to be positive to give a smile, so having a positive mindset is one aspect of smiling more, but it's also more than that. Smiling requires a generous and giving mindset. You have to be focused on someone other than yourself, even if it's just for a brief moment. Smiling tells the other person you are happy, and it's okay to be happy as well. It's already been scientifically proven that smiling helps spread happiness. That's why people don't regularly smile. Everyone is so focused on themselves and not willing to put that aside for a minute and think about doing something nice for someone else. Smiling has the power to help change someone's day and that can cause a chain reaction of positive interactions for the rest of the day. You never know how far your smile will go if you have just a little courage to give one.

A Summary of why you should smile more

- Neurotransmitters called endorphins are released when you smile. Endorphins help decrease stress. Believe it or not, they are also natural painkillers.

- Smiling literally makes you happy and builds a positive attitude

- Smiling helps you form naturally bonded relationships

3rd Law of Communication: A Crazy Simple Action That Makes You and Everyone Feel a Lot Better

This is the simplest thing you can do to boost your communication skills, and its shocking how many people don't do it! Kids and little children do this often, even some of your pets seem to be able to pull this off; but walk down the street and look at the majority of people; they'll have their eyes forward and faces straight. We're talking about the easy to do communication skill of smiling. Yes, smiling.

Smiling is a great way to leave a positive impression on others you communicate with. To smile is to be confident and this helps anyone you meet to automatically feel more comfortable. Smiling is a way to help put everyone around you at ease. It's even scientifically proven that smiling has a tremendous positive effect on you, as well as others around you.

The Science Behind Smiling

Smiling literally makes you happy. Researchers at the University of Munich used an MRI machine to measure the emotional processing receptors in the brain. They first measured people that smiled naturally. Then they took the second group, injected Botox into their cheeks to prevent them from smiling, and then again measure their brains. The scientists found that just the physical act of smiling actually activated the emotional happiness circuits in the brain!

Additional data showed that smiling was crucial in forming relationships. Individuals with brain lesions, physical malfunctions, physiological disorders and other similar conditions that led to the loss of facial control had more difficulty forming substantive relationships because they couldn't control the muscles to smile. Smiling is the first ingredient that brings two people together.

Having a smile on your face not only makes you happy, but also makes others happy as well. Researchers from Sweden exposed study participants to real and genuine smiles and measured their reactions. They found that genuine smiles received directly induced smiles from the participants. Smiling is contagious.

Many people are able to see someone's talent or natural abilities, but fail to actually tell them and praise them for it. Go the extra mile; see, and then speak out your praise and appreciation for people. Let someone know they are making a positive impression on you, not by directly saying it, but by complimenting them. Give others credit where credit is due and be generous with kind statements. This will have a great effect on you, as well as you will have more confidence in yourself just by giving that other person a little appreciation.

Acceptance

Another way for you to make someone feel important or valued is simply by accepting them. Acceptance does not have quite the same practical application like appreciation or asking questions. Acceptance of the other person is shaped by your attitude. Your mindset as you approach any conversation with anyone will determine the level of acceptance that person feels.

All of us have a desire to be accepted just as we are. Many of us hunger to just be able to relax, let our hair down and just be ourselves. In moments of crisis or trauma, sometimes the only thing we want is to just talk about what's going on in our lives. Even without a conscious thought, we all can be in this mode.

Give people the right and the opportunity to be themselves with you. If they are a little quirky or struggling emotionally with something, just let them be themselves. If you are a person who is always finding fault in someone else, or you're always suggesting ways to remedy someone else's problem, you can come off cold and uncaring. Many times, people just want their voice to be heard, and accepting them as they are is a wonderful way to make them feel valued and important. Your attitude of acceptance towards them is like an invisible room they can be themselves in. People will be grateful for your acceptance and it will go a long way in making sure they don't forget who you are.

Attitude and Action Again

As you have read, this law of communication requires both an adjustment in your attitude and your actions. That's why common sense laws like these are more difficult to implement than some imagine. It's not just about doing this or doing that, it's about changing the way you think, and what you believe in your heart. This is actually the real engine to implementing these laws of communication.

5th Law of Communication: If You Do This One Thing, People Will Naturally Think You Are Great

As we mentioned earlier, most people like to talk about themselves. It makes them feel important and noticed. So logically, what is the best way for you to keep them feeling important and valued? Keep them talking of course. And how is that done? By the powerful use of asking questions.

The simple idea is missed by nearly everyone who doesn't intentionally try to develop their conversation skills. It is a sure-fire way to boost your confidence and help build up the other person's self-esteem. Think about it in a simple way: everyone wants to feel important. When people talk about themselves, they want to know that what they have to say matters to someone. You ask effective questions to draw them out so they keep talking, which helps them to continue to feel valued and important. The end result is they see that you made them feel important, which boosts your personality and reputation as a great person. Now, this is not a conscious moment that everyone experiences, but it is a heart's natural reaction to feeling special. It all starts with asking questions.

One Simple Phrase

It doesn't take a rocket scientist to ask questions. With that being said, there is no denying that after the small talk ends, asking questions can be an awkward moment waiting to happen. The key is to always keep the conversation moving and help the person open up. As the conversation unfolds, the communication has a better chance of flowing.

One simple phrase that can keep things moving forward is "Oh really, why is that?" or "Oh really, tell me about that?" These simple phrases can do magic in keep the other person talking and moving the conversation. The art of conversation does not have to be as difficult or uncomfortable as we make it. Asking questions is as much about having confidence as speaking is. When it comes to asking the right questions, simple is better. The whole point of one simple phrase that you can repeat for any follow up question is to keep the other person talking long enough for you to find another question to ask. Think of it like a simple game. The game is to keep the other person talking and not say anything but a question for the first 5 minutes. If you find someone really wanting to talk, you may only have to ask that one simple phrase once.

A Great Learning Opportunity

One of the great things about learning how to ask effective questions is the tremendous opportunity it provides for you to learn for free. Think about all the education you could receive from all the potential people you could meet. There are endless opportunities all around to learn. Everyone you come in contact with can teach you something. Everyone has something to share and some form of wisdom to give. Think of the insight you could gain into a vast array of subjects that you never had any knowledge of. For instance, you love the making of films and you happen to meet a cinematographer. How much could you learn from him or her? Or you have a dream to be a writer and you meet a best-selling author. How could that help you? Or maybe you meet someone that does something that is just interesting to you because you have never heard about it before. In the end, the more you learn about things, the more you'll be able to connect with others. You won't have to talk about superficial topics, because you'll have a wealth of general knowledge about a wide variety of subjects from a wide variety of people. In asking questions, you could help connect people that could be valuable to one another. The possibilities really are endless; it's all because you asked a few simple questions to help someone else feel important.

Here are just a few points to remember about asking the right questions:

Ask Open Questions

An open question is what should provide you with in-depth answers. You can't answer open questions in two words or less. This also excludes "yes" and "no" responses. This is always your best bet with any question.

Open questions are usually connected with the Six "W's" Who? What? When? Where? Why? How?

Clarifying

Clarifying questions are probing questions. They are usually asked during a conversation to get a better understanding of what is being said. This requires careful attention to what the other person is saying, so that the right clarifying question can be asked and the conversation and topic can stay connected. Clarifying questions can also be asked after a conversation to rephrase and check that you understood everything clearly.

The smartest people in the world listen more than they talk. We'll cover more on listening in the next chapter, but the key to listening is having someone to listen to. That requires them to be talking and it's your job to ask good questions to keep them talking!

6th Law of Communication: How to Seem Clever Without Saying a Single Word

In the same way that asking questions and making someone feel important will make you seem better to the person you're talking with, listening has the same effect. This makes sense, given that you can't listen if you don't ask any questions to keep the other person talking. The two go hand in hand. When you listen, you encourage people to talk, making them feel important and even more so when they feel you are listening to them. It also works the other way around. Communication is a two-way street; if you want others to listen whenever you speak, you should be willing to give the same courtesy of listening to others.

Yes, listening. It is an important skill to have. After all, good communication skills require a high level of self-awareness. To be a really good communicator, you need to be aware of not just how well you engage others with your words, but how engaged you are when others talk to you. How well you listen and pay attention affects the quality of everything in your life. From your jobs to all of your relationships.

Why do we listen? To understand what's going on. To be able to enjoy what we hear. To learn new information. Listening creates confidence in you and connection with the other person; all without saying a single word.

Listening sounds easy, but research suggests that we only remember 25 to 50 percent of what we hear. That's because our brain can only handle a handful of things within our short term memory before it's stored away into our long term memory. Even when presented with information, you may not recall hearing the whole message. Your short term memory has limited space.

Because you can only remember so much, it certainly helps to improve your listening skills. By becoming a better listener, you improve productivity, your ability to influence and persuade others and you can avoid a lot of conflict in the future.

Active Listening

Active listening is where you make the conscious effort to hear not only the words someone else is saying, but also the message in its entirety. By practicing active listening, you can improve your listening skills substantially. In order to pull this off, you have to pay close attention to the other person. You can't become distracted by whatever else is happening. You cannot make counterarguments when they are done speaking. You cannot let your focus wander or grow bored.

If you find it hard to concentrate on what someone is saying, try repeating the words mentally as they talk. This will reinforce the message to you and keep you focused.

To enhance your listening skills, you need to let the other person know that you are listening to what they are saying. Ask yourself if you have ever been engaged in a conversation before, when you wondered if the other person was listening to you. Was your message getting across to them, or even worth speaking about? You obviously want to keep others engaged and not let them feel like they are talking to a brick wall.

Be sure to try and respond to the speaker in a way that will encourage him or her to continue speaking. Hence, the importance of the last chapter on asking questions. If you zone out or say nothing, they'll realize that you aren't listening and stop. So while you can nod and comment to show that you're interested, a question made during the talk, shows that you're paying attention and want to learn more.

To become a better active listener, there are five basic steps:

1. Pay Attention. Acknowledge the speaker's message, and remember that even non-verbal cues speak loudly. Keep your mind off distracting thoughts, avoid rebuttals and look at the speaker while they're talking. The biggest factor in being able to pay attention to someone is your eye contact with them. Look them in the eye and they will know you are paying attention.

2. Show That You're Listening. Acknowledgement can be something as simple as a nod of the head or a small "uh huh." You don't have to agree with the person, just simply show that you are listening. You can also use subtle signs like body language to show that you are listening.

3. Provide Feedback. What all speakers like to hear is some sort of comment to validate themselves; after all, wouldn't you like to hear someone give their opinion about what you were talking about? Just be sure to understand what is being said and try to avoid personal filters like judgment, assumptions and personal beliefs that could cause conflict. Reflect on what you are told and ask questions periodically. This can be either summarizing the speaker's comments or clarifying what they said. You could also ask for more information with a simple question.

4. Defer Judgment. Do not interrupt the speaker, even with counter arguments: It's frustrating, rude and hinders you from understanding the full message. Allow the speaker to finish every point they have before you start asking questions.

5. Respond Appropriately. Active listening is meant to be a model for respect and understanding. You gain information and perspective from it, and gain nothing by putting the speaker down. Be honest and open, but assert your responses and opinions respectively. Treat the speaker with respect.

To be an active listener, it takes a lot of concentration and determination. It might be hard because of old habits but it's worth it.

Be deliberate while listening and frequently remind yourself that your goal is to truly hear what the other person is saying. Put all your other thoughts and behaviors aside as you concentrate on the message. Ask, reflect and paraphrase so you can understand the message better.

7th Law of Communication: Follow This If You Want To Resolve Any Conflict

The last law of communication isn't so much about having confidence, or even being comfortable. It's really about being the best person you can be and learning how to grow in difficult and challenging times. This includes any time of conflict or distress when communicating with someone you care for.

Conflict will happen when you communicate. It doesn't matter if it is an acquaintance or a spouse, conflict can strike at any time. The biggest problem with any and all forms of communication is facing conflict of interests. Although it's not the most enjoyable process, it is a normal and healthy part of any relationship. When people fight or argue, it is on a disagreement they cannot simply overlook. Only by tackling the problems can the issues go away. In the end, conflict can even strengthen the bonds of a relationship because of the work and commitment involved in working through it.

Here are the basic principles of conflict resolution:

Affirm the relationship

Relationships are intangible but fragile bonds. They take a long time to build up, yet can be easily broken with the wrong words at the wrong time.

Conflicts between friends can happen when there is a difference in anything. Maybe you have said an opinion or done something offensive to upset the person, and vice versa. Even if the problems look and seem trivial, they matter if they have caused an argument. Conflicts on a whole trigger strong emotions to fester up, and are dangerous to ignore.

Do everything you can to maintain the relationship. Stay calm always, but not to the point of appearing distant or aloof. Keep your emotions in control to avoid making things worse. Take a quick break if you feel that it is necessary.

The biggest thing when it comes to conflict and resolving it is maintaining and affirming the relationship. Before any discussion and conflict resolution starts, you should affirm the relationship you have with the other person. Let them know that you care about them and want the best for your relationship. Compliment and praise your friend afterward to let them know how much your relationship with them means to you. This is easy to say, but harder to do in the midst of a heated discussion. Just remember to do everything you can to make sure the other person knows that your relationship is important. This will go a long way in making you and whoever you are talking with, feel more secure and safe as you have those difficult conversations.

Seek to understand

There is never a better time to be empathetic than when a conflict between you and someone close builds. Everyone *needs* to feel understood and supported. They *need* to feel like they are important to someone, but those needs vary from person to person. What is helpful and comfortable to one person may not be as comfortable for someone else.

Any conflict is usually a difference of what someone wants or what someone expects. It's okay for others to have different wants or expectations, but it's important to remember that those varying needs and desires are what really cause the conflict. Many times, the service level argument is really a sign of a deeper need or desire that isn't being met. When those situations come up, it's important for you to first seek to understand the other person. Use the law of asking questions to clarify the issues. Allow the other person their turn to talk openly and do not react negatively or get defensive. Stay calm and composed. One basic principle of communication is that others will often mirror your reactions. If you are yelling, it's almost an automatic response that the other person will yell. So allow the opportunity for you to seek to understand. No matter what happens, stay calm and just listen. This is a crucial steps towards resolving the issue.

Seek to be understood

This is your opportunity to share your feelings; however, the opportunity may only come up if you've done your part in first seeking to understand the other person. Empathy is a two-way street, but someone has to be the bigger person and allow the other a chance to be heard. This helps to give you the chance to share your feelings and how you are approaching the conflict. Make sure you aren't usually throwing any accusations, and simply refer to your feelings. Don't respond with "you made me," or "you always do this…" Confine in your thoughts, state your feelings. Let them know what you want and maybe you can figure something out.

Own responsibility

Most conflict resolves around placing the blame on someone else. The blame game gets tossed back and forth and everyone continues to hurl accusations and regretful words at one another.

Nothing will help resolve conflict and ease tension more than taking responsibility. When you take 100% responsibility for your situation, you literally diffuse the conflict bomb. If you own up to what happened, there is no one to blame. The other person can't blame you because you are already fully aware of what you did and you're owning up to it. This is the secret to faster and smoother conflict resolution. Just ask yourself this question, "How am I responsible here?" There is always an answer. You will never ask that question and not have an answer that can help you overcome your conflict, but you have to be willing to be humble and swallow your pride.

Seek agreement

Try to be as diplomatic and understanding as possible. Listen to what is being said, and try to make the resolution a priority. Everyone always wants to be "right", and if everyone DOES want to be right in an argument, it'll never resolve itself.

Even if you can't come to an agreement on how to resolve the issue, agree to disagree. Arguments and conflicts only continue if two or more people are still at it. This may require compromise. Don't try to keep score on how much you have done for the person or how little they have done for you. If your target is resolving the conflict, then it shouldn't be as difficult to come to some sort of agreement.

Conflicts and arguments can also be very draining, so learn to pick your battles. Ask yourself; is this fight worth it? What do you want out of it? Do you want to prove something, or is it just to satisfy your ego?

Praise the slightest improvement

It is so easy to just act on anger when you are upset or slighted, but there are healthier ways to respond to conflict; being rational enough to recognize and respond to things that matter; making calm and non-defensive reactions; having the readiness to forgive and forget and moving on without resentment, as well as seeking compromise and avoiding punishment.

If you have both agreed to change for the better, make sure they know about it. For every little change or improvement they make, make sure you celebrate that. Your growth and the other person's growth are positive steps to having a better relationship and it also decreases the chances you'll argue over that specific issue again.

Change is not easy; neither is living in constant conflict. With a little effort and determination though, resolving conflict can lead to a happier relationship and a happier life. Here's to better days ahead for you!

Conclusion

Thank you again for purchasing this book!

I hope this book was able to help you learn how to be a good communicator and have confidence in doing it!

The next step is to decide to put all those skills you learned to the test. Back at the third chapter, there was an assignment for you to go out and greet everyone with at least a smile. That's a good first step. From there, try to improve your listening skills with your peers and family. Ask how their days were, ask some clarifying questions and try to recall what they did. Take one new principle and take a small action, one step at a time!

Finally, if you enjoyed this book, please take the time to share your thoughts and post a review on Amazon. It'd be greatly appreciated!

Thank you and good luck!

P.S-Don't forget to check out your FREE BONUS on the next page! You won't want to miss out on it!

Also check out my other books from the "7 Laws" Series on success and personal growth on the last page!

FREE BONUS E-BOOK!

Body Language Mastery

How would you like to control your actions to the point where you are exuding confidence and belief in yourself? What about being able to help someone open up to you on an interview or a first date? Do you want to be able to create any type of positive reaction, without saying a word? Master human psychology by reading the way people behave with their bodies...

briancagneey.com/bodylanguagemasterybook

OTHER BOOKS IN THE "7 LAWS" SERIES

Check out the current and upcoming books in Brian Cagneey's "7 Laws" series on personal development and success!

http://amazon.com/author/briancagneey

The 7 Laws Of Habits: Using Habits To Achieve Success, Happiness And Anything You Want!

The 7 Laws Of Motivation: Explode Your Motivation And Create A Mindset Built For Success

The 7 Laws Of Happiness: Using The Power Of Happiness To Create Amazing Results In Life!

The 7 Laws Of Productivity: 10X Your Success With Focus, Time Management, Self-Discipline And Action.

The 7 Laws Of Fear: Break What's Holding You Back And Turn Fear Into Confidence.

The 7 Laws of Confidence: Feel Unstoppable, Destroy Doubt And Accomplish Your Biggest Goals.

The 7 Laws Of Focus: Focus: The #1 Secret For Excellence, Productivity and Radical Results.

The 7 Laws Of Leadership: Develop Yourself, Influence Others And People Will Follow.

The 7 Laws of Communication: The Secrets Of Being Comfortable, Confident And Unforgettable With Anyone!

The 7 Laws Of Self-Discipline: Become Strong, Become Confident And Create Your Success

The 7 Laws Of Coaching: Powerful Coaching Skills That Will Predict Your Team's Success

http://amazon.com/author/briancagneey

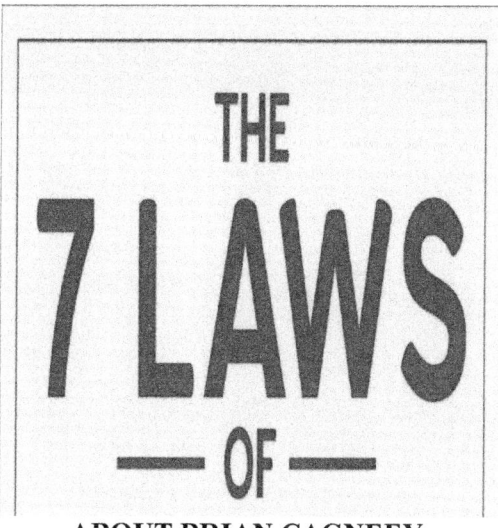

ABOUT BRIAN CAGNEEY

Brian Cagneey is the author of the well-known "7 Laws" book series on personal development. His books cover a wide range of topics including personal growth, habits, self-discipline, happiness, success, communication, leadership, coaching, motivation, confidence, fear, productivity and focus.

Brian's mission is to renew people's minds and to help every day, ordinary people become positive, successful and mission driven. His passion for writing is fueled by the desire to see as many people as possible not just survive their life, but thrive and excel.

Brian is an avid student of the laws of success. His beliefs on accomplishment are not based on theory, but real life practice. Brian knows that wisdom and knowledge are only half of the equation; the other half of success is taking massive amounts of action over a sustained period of time.

"Anyone can succeed with the ultimate principle of success: small, consistent action over a long period of time. If anyone can master that law through focus, self-discipline and confidence, there isn't anything that's impossible to accomplish."

Check out the other book in the "7 Laws" series today!

amazon.com/author/briancagneey